First of all, I want to begin this book by offering you my sincere condolences for the loss of your pet.
Let's take a moment together to share a loving thought for him.

Now, I welcome you

Our paths cross today because y

tragedy that I have also experienced. the loss of your loyal companion.

Do you feel like you've lost everything?
Do you feel like there's no way out?
Do you think you'll never be happy again?
I know what you're going through.

You're slowly sinking into anxiety, despair, guilt, and you can't seem to soothe the pain.
That's normal — you're going through a natural process tied to the loss of your companion, a process known as pet grief.

I have good news for you. You're in the right place.
Here, you will be guided, understood, and most importantly, never judged.

This book will guide you step by step toward the healing and peace you're seeking.

It will serve as a companion, helping you become aware of the different stages you're going through.

You'll have the space to write down everything you find difficult to express and begin to build a soothing dialogue with yourself.

In this book, we will work together — but only you can be the main actor in your own healing journey.

Do you know why?

Because it's important to understand that there is no miracle cure when grieving.

But know this: the answers lie within you.

I'm here to help you accept your negative emotions, because trying to fight them is exhausting.

And for you to get the most out of this book, I strongly encourage you to reflect on and answer all the questions.

Trust yourself — because I trust you.

I know you'll do things the right way, because deep down, you truly want to feel better.

Table of Contents.

The Human–Animal Relationship.

A Bit of History.

The relationship between humans and animals has evolved greatly over time.

Originally, this relationship was based solely on predation. Humans hunted animals for food.

Later, in order to meet their nutritional needs, humans began to domesticate animals for farming — such as sheep, cattle, chickens, ducks, and pigs.

Gradually, humans started to form special bonds with certain animals.
The horse, for example, became both a means of transport and a valuable helper in daily agricultural tasks.

Dogs also held a special place early on, particularly among the wealthy, where they were used for hunting and guarding property.

It was only after the Industrial Revolution that these relationships truly changed.

Work and livestock farming gave way to leisure and domestication.

Anthropomorphism.

Today, **more than 50%** of the world's population owns at least one pet. The role of animals in our homes has taken on an entirely new dimension — to the point where they've become full-fledged members of the **family**.

If you're reading this book today, that was probably your case. You saw your pet as your baby, the child, sibling, or best friend you never had — or even as your confidant when you had no one else to talk to.

Your pet may have lived in your home and shared a large part of your daily life and personal space. So, what could be more natural than considering them part of your family?

Just like a child, you gave them a name, fed them, trained them, and took care of them. You probably gave them gifts at Christmas or on their birthday. Maybe you even used "**baby talk**" — that tender, affectionate way of speaking with loving nicknames.

This phenomenon is called **anthropomorphism**.
And there's no shame in it — quite the opposite.
It shows that you have a big heart, and that your pet was lucky to have you as their guardian.

In what ways was your pet a precious member of your family?

Tell me about the moments that shaped your bond.

_____

_____

_____

_____

_____

_____

The Role and Benefits of Pets.

Today, animals play many roles in our households.

Here are the main ones:

- Companionship

As the name suggests, a pet is above all a **companion**.
They are a **remedy for loneliness** and a **comforting presence**
that listens without judgment, no matter the worries.

- Health

Animals help **improve our health**.
They provide a sense of well-being that slows down breathing,
lowers blood pressure, and reduces heart rate.
So much so that **the risk of cardiovascular disease is reduced
by 25 to 30%**.
They are also powerful therapeutic tools.
Their positive impact is used in the treatment of certain
illnesses, including serious conditions such as leukemia, cancer,
and psychosis.
Their presence helps vulnerable individuals and reduces stress.
This is known as animal-assisted therapy, or **zootherapy**.

Let's take the example of **purr therapy**, the idea that a cat's purring emits sound frequencies with a calming effect.

Likewise, aquariums — often found in hospitals — help create a soothing and reassuring atmosphere.

- Responsibility

Having a pet inevitably requires the owners to take on responsibility.
They are in charge of the animal's health, nutrition, and overall well-being.

Pets also have a very positive impact on a child's development.
Even at a young age, a child can be responsible for small tasks related to their pet's care — such as feeding, brushing, or walking them.
Through this, the child learns empathy and builds self-confidence.
Losing a pet is often a child's first experience with grief.
As painful as it may be, this kind of loss is an important milestone in their emotional growth.
(The topic of pet loss in children is explored in detail in a later section of this book.)

- Assistance/Work

Some animals — especially dogs — provide invaluable help in the lives of many people.

Guard dogs, hunting dogs, herding dogs, guide dogs for the blind, police dogs, and service dogs are just a few examples.

Horses and livestock also assist with transportation and agricultural work.

This list of the roles and benefits of animals is by no means exhaustive, and it's up to each person to recognize the unique role their own pet plays in their life.

Describe three roles your pet played in your life:

1. ....

....

....

2. ....

....

....

3. ....

....

....

What Is Pet Bereavement?

Pet bereavement is a natural process that occurs after the loss of a beloved companion.

It is a journey — shorter or longer depending on the individual — that unfolds step by step with the goal of accepting the loss and finding peace again.

It has nothing to do with forgetting your pet — quite the opposite.

I often compare it to the healing of a wound.
It's a process that takes place after an injury.
It's **natural** and **necessary**, and its duration varies depending on the severity or depth of the wound.

During grief, it's completely normal to experience a wide range of symptoms such as anger, fear, a need for comfort, a loss of interest in the outside world, guilt, and above all, deep sadness and a feeling of injustice.

The ultimate goal of this process is to allow you to hold on to the love and the memories, which will remain forever etched in your heart.

It is at this point that you will feel joyful and at peace once again.

You could also say that it will help you create an unbreakable inner bond with your departed companion.

I find these quotes especially beautiful and meaningful, so I wanted to share them with you:

"Grief is the price we pay for love."
— Queen Elizabeth II

"You are no longer where you were, but you are everywhere I am."
— Victor Hugo

"Healing is never as swift as the wound."
— Folk wisdom

"In the end, it's not the years in your life that count. It's the life in your years."
— Abraham Lincoln

The Impact of Losing a Pet

The loss of a pet is still a taboo subject today, often misunderstood by society.

The pain felt when a pet passes away is immense — yet those around us, often with good intentions but clumsy words, tend to minimize the loss.

There is a clear lack of support and understanding compared to the death of a human being.

What you are experiencing in your grief is what I call a double misunderstanding:

There is the shock of losing your pet, which brings emotional confusion (we resist accepting such an unbearable reality), and at the same time, you're forced to face society's lack of understanding.

This makes the grieving process much more difficult.

You've probably already heard phrases that no one would dare say to you after the loss of a human loved one:

"It's nothing, you can always adopt another pet."

"It's not a big deal."

"Don't worry, it's just an animal."

"You'll feel better tomorrow, it'll pass."

"Why are you making such a big deal out of it?"

"You shouldn't get so attached to an animal."

These "words" only worsen your wounds.
They minimize the significance of your loss and do nothing to ease your pain — quite the opposite.

Having recently lost my own cat at just six years old, I can tell you from experience that the unconditional love our companions give us — and that we give them in return — truly deserves a grief that is honored and respected.

"I Feel Ridiculous"

If you feel ridiculous for mourning your pet, allow me to remind you that loving is **never** ridiculous.

Very often, when you try to share what you're feeling with others, you're met with misunderstanding or **judgment** — as if your grief doesn't carry enough weight to be taken seriously. As if mourning an animal were something childish. It can be deeply unsettling to feel misunderstood, as though the pain you're experiencing is being dismissed or minimized.

But the truth is, those who don't understand you likely never had the **chance** to experience a deep, heartfelt bond with an animal.
They may have never felt that kind of **profound love** — and so, they're simply not capable of truly understanding what you're going through.

Just because others don't understand doesn't make your grief any less **valid**. What you're feeling is not exaggerated or abnormal.
It's the reflection of a unique bond — a friendship that left a lasting imprint on your **heart**. Animals ask for nothing but love, and in return, they offer a kind of affection so pure that few human relationships can compare to such a connection.

No matter if others don't understand the importance of that relationship — you know how much it meant, and that's what truly matters. The pain you're feeling now is a measure of the love you gave and received. So no, your sorrow doesn't make you ridiculous — it simply makes you **deeply human**, with sincere and **meaningful** emotions.

"It's Just an Animal"

This is a phrase we often hear when we're looking for comfort.

Our loved ones minimize our pain by saying it was "**just**" an animal — that there are others, that it's better to lose a pet than a human loved one, or worse: that you can simply buy another one.

But let me tell you something else: it wasn't just an animal — it was your best friend. A unique being with their own personality, their own name, their own character. In short, a true member of your family.

And they deserve to be mourned with dignity, because I can assure you: you will never heal by minimizing your grief.

It's sad to say, but... others can't truly understand what you're feeling — because the bond you created with your companion is one of a kind. And you are the only one who can fully understand it.

So stop seeking comfort from those who don't get it. Because instead of soothing you, their words may only frustrate or upset you — and offer nothing truly helpful in return.

Have you ever been confronted with hurtful comments?
If so, write them down here.

....

....

....

Describe how your loved ones reacted when you told
them the news.

....

....

....

What were you hoping to receive from them?

....

....

....

"I Would Have Been Better Off Never Having a Pet"

You might find yourself thinking this — because you're hurting.

The pain and grief are overwhelming, and they may lead you to believe that the connection wasn't worth it.

That feeling is understandable, but it only deepens your sorrow.
Let me share my perspective — a stoic and positive one:
The pain you're feeling right now is nothing compared to the years of **joy** you shared with your pet.

Do you know why?

Because that's what **life** is: we laugh, we cry, we live, we die.
Without the lows, there can be no highs — and without the highs, there would be no lows.

In other words: meeting your pet brought **richness** and **love** into your life.

If you had never met their gaze, your life would have been a little **flatter**, a little less meaningful.

So instead of holding on to the sadness of this loss, try to turn it into **gratitude** for all the beautiful moments you shared together.

Because I promise you, the period of grief is always insignificant compared to the thousands of moments and memories we create with these little beings.

So be **happy** and **proud**!

Happy to have known your companion.

Happy to have known love.

Proud to have been their protector.

Proud to have made them happy by giving them a life filled with love every single day.

Happy to have shared such special moments together.
That's what real life is all about.

So yes, right now — as you read this book — you're heartbroken. And so what? This grief is temporary. One day, this pain will turn into beautiful memories and give way to the rainbow.

Don't you think it's better to suffer because you loved... than to suffer because you never did?

In the next chapter, I'd like us to explore the different stages of grief together — so that you can finally experience it fully, and without guilt.

The Stages of Pet Grief.

An animal's life cycle is shorter than ours.

In most cases, and in the natural order of things, our companions leave before we do. Over the course of our lives, we will often love and lose more than one animal.

Grief is a path you must absolutely walk.
It's a unique journey, one that blends pain with memories.

But it's not a journey you have to take alone.

You can rely on this guide to bring you comfort and help restore hope in the face of the deep sadness that's overwhelming you.

Just like with human grief, pet grief unfolds in different stages.

Each of these stages is important for your healing and may last for varying lengths of time — from a few days to several months.

Grief becomes complicated or unhealthy when you remain stuck in one stage and can't find a way to move forward.

Let me walk you through each of these stages.

The Stages of Pet Grief.

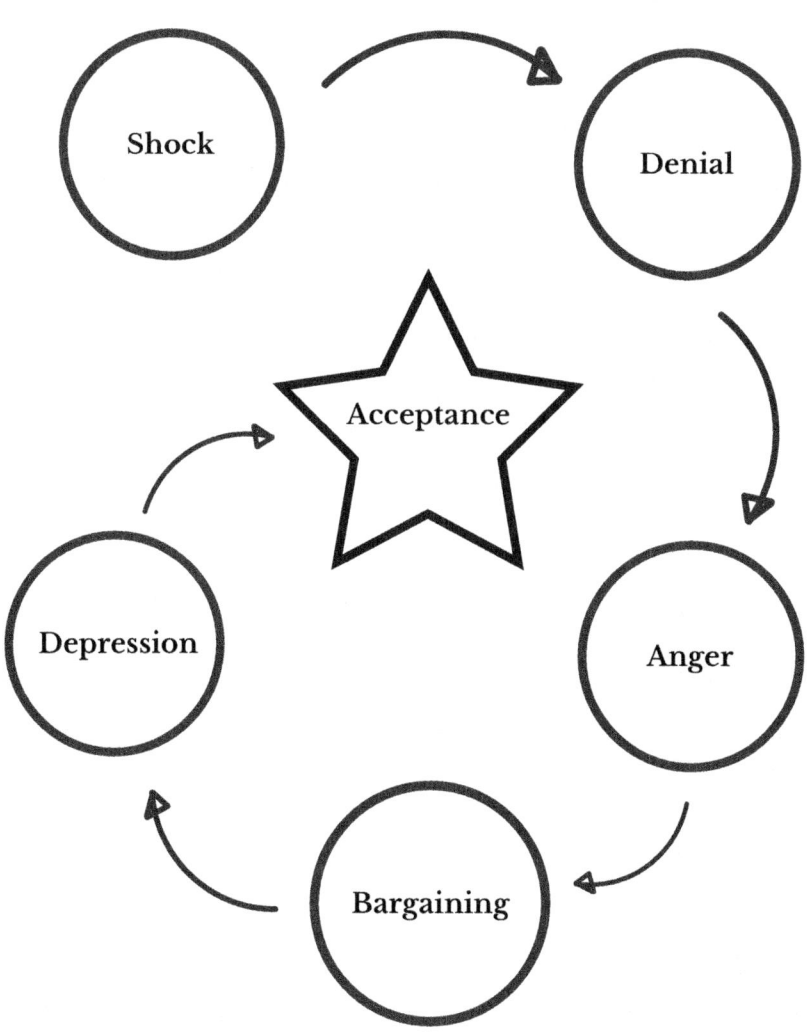

Shock.

This is your first reaction to the loss.
As the name suggests, this stage can be quite intense —
depending largely on how sudden the death was.

An accident or a sudden illness will usually cause a much more
powerful shock than a long-term illness or a natural death due
to old age.

During this stage, your body is overwhelmed with intense
emotions. You may feel the urge to scream, shout, cry.
You might experience nausea, trembling, or a tightness in your
chest. In some cases, it can even lead to panic attacks or fainting.

It's important that you allow these reactions to happen and find
a way to release them. Do not hold back your screams or your
tears out of shame or modesty.

In some situations, shock may instead take the form of silence
— an emotional numbness, a complete lack of visible reaction.
This shouldn't be mistaken for a lack of empathy or love for
your pet.

It's simply a natural defense mechanism your body uses to
protect you, to temporarily distance you from the most painful
emotions. This response allows you to slowly begin to process
the reality of your loss.

A similar phenomenon occurs when you are seriously injured.

Typically, you don't feel the pain right away.

The adrenaline released during the accident temporarily masks your pain.

Your body focuses on protecting your vital organs to keep you alive.

Denial.

This stage can happen at the same time as shock.

It manifests as a refusal to accept reality.

You behave as if your companion were still alive.

You cling to the belief that there's been a mistake and avoid talking about their death.

You imagine they'll come back and that life will return to how it was.

"This can't be happening!"

"It's just a nightmare — I'm going to wake up!"

...these are the kinds of thoughts running through your mind.

Just like with shock, this stage — filled with irrational thoughts — is a defense mechanism for the mind.

It delays full awareness and allows you to process the loss more gradually.

In most cases, the shock and denial stages are short-lived.

What was the cause of their passing?

....

....

....

....

What was your first reaction to the loss of your pet?

....

....

....

....

Anger.

The harsh reality eventually catches up with you, triggering a deep sense of anger.

The shock and confusion begin to fade, and you slowly come to realize what has happened — and that nothing can turn back time.
You have no choice but to **face** your loss.

You feel a strong sense of **injustice**.

Why did this have to happen to you and not someone else?

You believe your pet didn't deserve to go.

You get angry at fate, at the god you believe in, or more broadly — at life itself.

You feel irritable, and a deep frustration follows you throughout the day. You may even find yourself feeling jealous of people whose pets are still alive and well.

You look for someone to blame — maybe the vet, your loved ones, or even yourself.
In fact, in many cases, this anger is accompanied by a strong sense of **guilt**.

"Maybe the vet didn't make the right diagnosis or waited too long to act."

"It's my fault!"

"If I had done things differently, they would still be here today!"

This guilt is difficult to manage and may stay with you through several stages.
But believe me — it will eventually **ease**.

It's important to release this anger.
Surround yourself with people who know you well, who understand and support you, because they know this anger is simply an expression of your pain.

I encourage you to engage in physical activity — something that allows you to let off steam and clear your mind.

I also invite you to put your anger into words.
Write down everything that comes to mind.
You can blame, curse, shout on paper — let that resentment out.
You'll feel **lighter** afterward.

Who are you angry with?

How does anger show up in you?

"He didn't deserve to die".

You tell yourself that your pet was innocent, defenseless, and didn't deserve to leave so soon. You wonder why it had to happen to your companion and not someone else's.

Your emotions are absolutely valid, but they also intensify your grief and create a powerful feeling of injustice within you.

Know this: no one "deserves" to die.
Because life isn't about what we deserve.
Life is an adventure — and its end is inevitable.
Thanks to you, your pet lived the most beautiful adventure, and that's something you can truly be **proud of**.

Your companion was loved, protected, and surrounded with kindness. You always did your best to offer them your love, your presence, and your devotion.

That's exactly what they did deserve — and you were there for them, right until the very end.

So don't stay stuck on the injustice of their loss.
Don't focus only on the ending — instead, try to hold on to the countless joyful moments you shared. Because what truly matters is the Love — with a capital L — that you both experienced.

That love is indelible. And it will **never end**.

Bargaining.

This is a more "spiritual" or illusory phase, linked to the feeling of powerlessness you experience in the face of your pet's death.

The anxiety this creates leads you to try to "negotiate" with yourself — hence the term bargaining.

Your mind tries to find ways to reverse what happened.
There is still hope, deep down, that things could go back to how they were.
You start wondering what you could have done to bring them back. You imagine scenarios that might have prevented the outcome, such as:

"What would've happened if..."

"If I had taken them to another vet..."

"If I had listened to that person..."

"If I hadn't listened to that person..."

How does bargaining show up in you?

You're still living in the past — in a reality where your pet is still with you. You find yourself caught in repetitive thoughts about the events that happened before their death.

What if I had consulted
another vet?

Why didn't I notice he
was suffering before it
was too late?

If I had listened to my
intuition...

If I had seen that he was
sick, maybe I could have
done something.

If I had made the
decision to euthanize
him sooner, he wouldn't
have suffered as much.

If I had done things
differently, he might
still be here.

Did I do everything I
could for him, or did I
miss something?

Did I comfort him
enough before he
passed?

This phase is normal, and these thoughts are completely natural. Remind yourself that you did your best with the information you had at that moment.

Unfortunately, we can't always anticipate what's going to happen.

Know that this stage is often short-lived.

I strongly encourage you to express everything you're feeling to those around you.

Do you know why?

Because everything you say, you release.
Let those negative thoughts out instead of burying them inside.
That's the key. And patience will be your greatest ally.

Remember, like all the other stages, this one is just a passage — a necessary part of your grief journey.

"Death, that thing we wish didn't exist, but that gives life all its meaning."

Do you imagine scenarios that could have prevented their death?

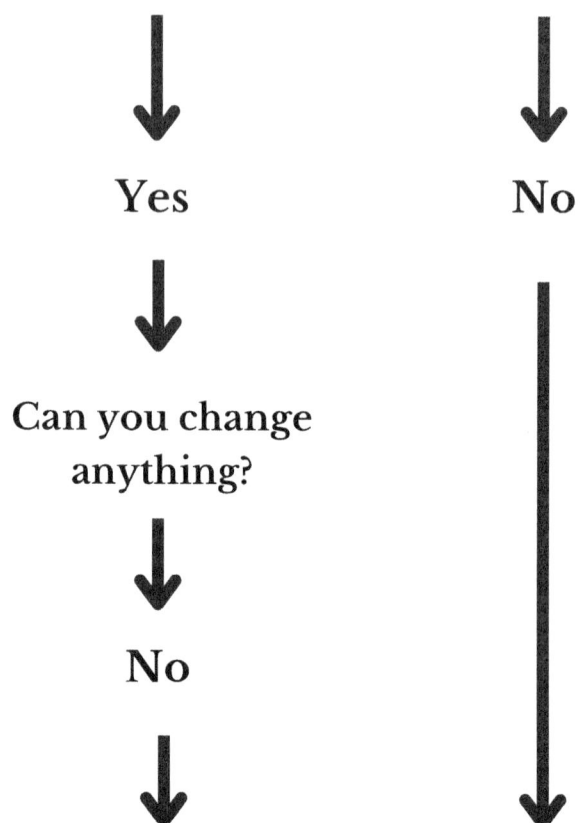

Yes

No

Can you change anything?

No

Then accept the past so you can appreciate the present.

Pain and Depression.

Pain.

It is inevitable and often difficult to cope with, as it can last a long time — but know that it is **necessary**.

Symptoms such as frequent crying, feelings of guilt, or despair about the future are common. You may feel alone and lost. That's normal. You need to find a way to release your emotions, because you've lost your sense of balance.

Naturally, you may start looking through photos and reliving countless memories. That's perfectly okay — it's not a bad sign. In fact, it marks the beginning of the grieving "**digestion**" process. There are different types of emotional pain depending on how you lost your pet, and that will affect the way you experience grief. Some losses are more difficult to process and accept than others.

1. Anticipatory Grief

You know this kind of pain when you've lost an elderly companion, when they passed away after a known illness, or when euthanasia was the most compassionate choice. This type of death is often easier to accept. You were fortunate enough to have time to prepare for their passing, and you were able to say goodbye.

2. Immediate Pain

Immediate pain occurs when death is sudden and unexpected.
Unlike anticipatory grief, you didn't have time to prepare for
the tragedy or say goodbye.
You know this kind of pain if your companion passed away in
an accident, for example.
This type of loss is especially difficult to accept because it feels
so illogical. You never imagined this would happen.

3. Complex Pain

Complex pain is the third type you may experience, for
example in the case of a sudden euthanasia or accidental death.
In these situations, guilt often plays a major role — you may
feel as though you are responsible for your pet's death.
This kind of pain complicates the grieving process because you
replay the events over and over, imagining different outcomes.
You experience deep trauma because the situation was so
abrupt and violent.

If you are suffering after a traumatic loss and find yourself
feeling constantly guilty, know that what you're going through is
normal — but please, be kind to yourself.
Instead of asking yourself what you could have done differently,
ask yourself what you did right for your pet throughout their
life.

"I Feel Responsible for Their Death"

If this phrase feels like it's stuck to your skin, then read the following carefully.

This sentence actually shows just how much you wanted the best for your pet. It proves that you were a deeply caring and attentive guardian. Isn't that true?

Yes, your companion is no longer here — that's the painful reality.

But remember: accidents remind us that our pets face daily risks and dangers that you have **no control** over.

It's easier to blame yourself than to accept that they were exposed to risks beyond your reach.

So yes, you're experiencing intense pain — but try to realize that you cannot take back control. What happened was a risk. One you may have never considered — but it was there nonetheless. And most importantly, it was beyond your control and not your fault.

You are not responsible. Their death was not something you caused. You always did what you could, and what was best for them — and they knew that.

We simply can't control everything.

Their life — just like ours — is made up of events, and some of them are completely beyond our will. So I encourage you to accept the past in order to better live in the present.

What type of pain are you experiencing?

Tell me what hurts you the most today.

How did you contribute to giving them a happy and fulfilling life?

Depression.

This is, without a doubt, the most painful stage of grief — but also the most important.

Why? Because you've come to understand that your companion is not coming back. You're living in the **present** again, and that's what makes you feel so alone.
This "discouragement phase" is marked by deep sadness, often accompanied by tears.
Everything feels dark. You've lost your sense of purpose.

"Why should I even get out of bed in the morning?"

You tell yourself that life no longer has meaning without them, and you may feel the urge to isolate yourself because you've lost your emotional compass.

You may experience the following:

- Physical symptoms
Crying, nausea, migraines, heart palpitations, stomach pain, numbness, difficulty breathing.

- Behavioral symptoms
Sleep disturbances, irritability, eating disorders, memory loss, social withdrawal, lack of motivation, difficulty making decisions or concentrating, craving comfort, feeling unsafe.

-    Emotional symptoms

Guilt, anger, anxiety, fear, helplessness, sadness, despair.

The term "depression" should be put into perspective.

This isn't a depression caused by a mental disorder, but rather a **reactive** — and above all **natural** — response to a painful and overwhelming event.
Even though this phase of depression is the longest and most painful, it is temporary.

It's by going through this deep sadness and despair that you will gradually be able to fully process the loss.
It's very important not to fight the emotions we've just listed — but to **welcome** them.

I strongly encourage you to surround yourself with others and seek support, because you'll need to release your pain and feel heard.

At first, you may not want to listen to what others have to say. But as you move forward in this stage, you'll slowly begin to accept their words.

"Talking about one's sorrows is already a way of consoling them." — Albert Camus

The Physical and Emotional Symptoms of Grief.

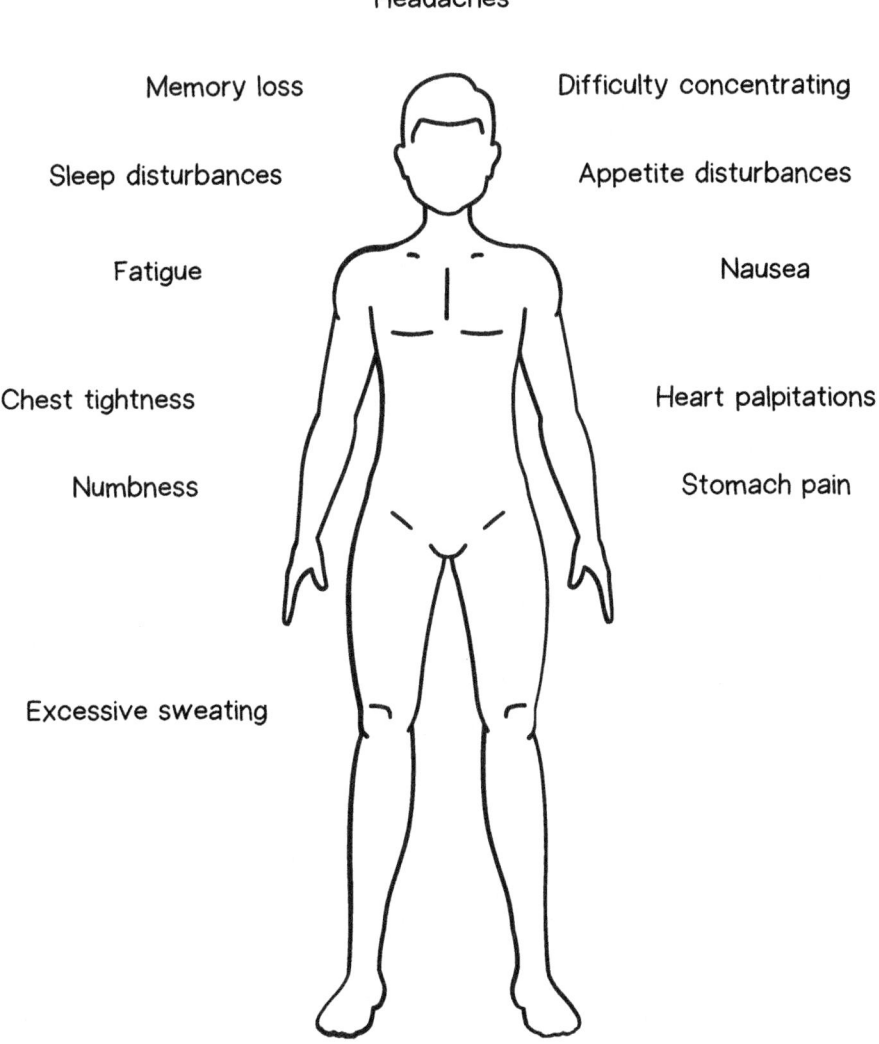

Headaches

Memory loss

Difficulty concentrating

Sleep disturbances

Appetite disturbances

Fatigue

Nausea

Chest tightness

Heart palpitations

Numbness

Stomach pain

Excessive sweating

Name three symptoms you're experiencing right now.

....

Are you crying?

....

What do you do to calm your tears?

....

What helps soothe your pain?

....

What makes your pain worse?

....

"Euthanasia: An Act of Love"

If you, like me, are asking yourself whether you made the right choice — or if you could have done things differently when the vet suggested euthanasia — then read carefully what I'm about to tell you.

Making the decision to put a beloved pet to sleep is one of the most **heartbreaking** choices we face in life, and I know how hard it is to bear. But it's important to remember one essential truth: you didn't make that decision lightly — you acted in their best interest, and most importantly, out of **love**.

Choosing to end your pet's suffering means you had the strength to offer them **peace**, at a time when life no longer meant comfort. It is a **selfless** act: you chose to ease their pain, putting aside your own desire to keep them with you.

It's a sign of pure and **courageous** love.

In time, guilt will give way to **gratitude**:

Gratitude for the chance you had to share part of your life with them. Gratitude for having known what it means to truly love an animal. And above all, gratitude for having been there for them until the very end. That love — that's what they felt until their final breath. So be at peace with this truth: your pet was loved until the end, and they did not suffer. They will always live in your heart — not through the pain of parting, but through all the beautiful memories you shared.

Remember: you showed the deepest form of **respect**, generosity, and love by standing by their side and ensuring they didn't suffer. So be proud of yourself.

41

Acceptance.

This is the final stage of the long path toward healing —
A phase of awareness.
The closing step, and the return to **reality**.

You're now beginning to **accept** your pet's passing, and you're
starting to feel better.
Little by little, you learn how to live in this new world — without
your companion.

You begin to build new routines, and you're once again able to
feel **joy** and **pleasure**, even if some sadness still arises when you
think of them.
You remember both the good times and the difficult ones you
shared together.

You know you've reached this healing phase when:

- You no longer try to place blame.
- You can look at photos and remember them without feeling
deep pain.
- You can talk about them without having an overwhelming
emotional reaction.
- You recall the happy memories — not just the painful ones.

"Nothing is more alive than a memory." — Federico García
Lorca

Little by little, you begin to enjoy the moments when you recall your memories. You look back on the past and recognize how lucky you were to have known that animal.

You speak of them with nostalgia — but no longer with unbearable pain.

Accepting this truth — death — gives you the ability to appreciate life even more deeply.

Because yes, acceptance is the greatest **power** a person can have. It is your greatest power.

Acceptance acts like armor.
It protects you from the blows of the outside world and allows you to feel **calm** and at **peace** with the reality of loss.

But be careful — acceptance does not mean forgetting your pet or fully "getting over" the loss.
It means learning to live with the pain,
finding joy again, and feeling peace return.

This stage will bring you great **resilience** in facing life's most difficult trials.

"No one can reach dawn without first walking the path of night."
— Khalil Gibran

As you've seen here, overcoming grief happens in several stages — and it doesn't happen overnight.

Don't be too hard on yourself, and above all, don't lose hope.

No one knows better than you what you're feeling — and if it affects you, then it matters.
Period.

So welcome and accept your pain — that's how healing begins.

Some people may find themselves stuck in one stage, which can lead to complicated grief.

If you feel like your grief is intensifying after 12 months, if your pain feels even stronger than at the beginning, if you're overwhelmed and stuck in a pathological state without making progress, I encourage you to seek help from a professional.

They can identify where you're blocked and help you move forward in the healthiest way possible.

Finding Comfort in Our Memories.

The silence after loss is devastating — it feels like you're being crushed by the weight of grief. But in that vast emptiness lies something no one can ever take away from you: your **memories**.

You shared so many beautiful moments — your first meeting, your daily routines, your walks, your holidays...
All of that will remain etched in your memory **forever**.
They are true treasures — untouched by time.

Memories are the **fruit of the love** they gave us.
They remind us that they were here, that we were lucky to meet them — and even luckier to share months, maybe even years, by their side. What more could we ask for?

By embracing this way of seeing things, your memories will gradually become a source of comfort.
You'll no longer say, "What a tragedy to have to live without them," but rather, "What a blessing it was to have lived with them."

I'm not saying it's easy, or that you'll shift your mindset overnight — because even as I write these words, I feel a pang in my heart thinking of my own animal.

But I just want you to know that one day, **gratitude** will outweigh the pain — not because you'll forget your pet, but because you'll realize that having known them was a true gift. So hold onto those memories — in the right way. Tell yourself that the bond isn't broken, it's simply transformed. Because even if they're no longer here, they're still watching over you.
Wipe your tears... and thank them.

Because thanks to them, your life will be **forever paw-printed**.

Tell me your most beautiful memory with your pet.

....

....

What are you most proud of in your grief journey?

....

....

If you had to choose three words that you learned by living
alongside your pet, what would they be?

....

....

If you had to help a grieving loved one, what advice would
you give them?

....

....

Painful memories will, with time, give way to joyful ones. Rather than being a source of sorrow, your memories will become an **emotional treasure** — keeping your pet's memory alive and reminding you of the richness of the moments you shared together.

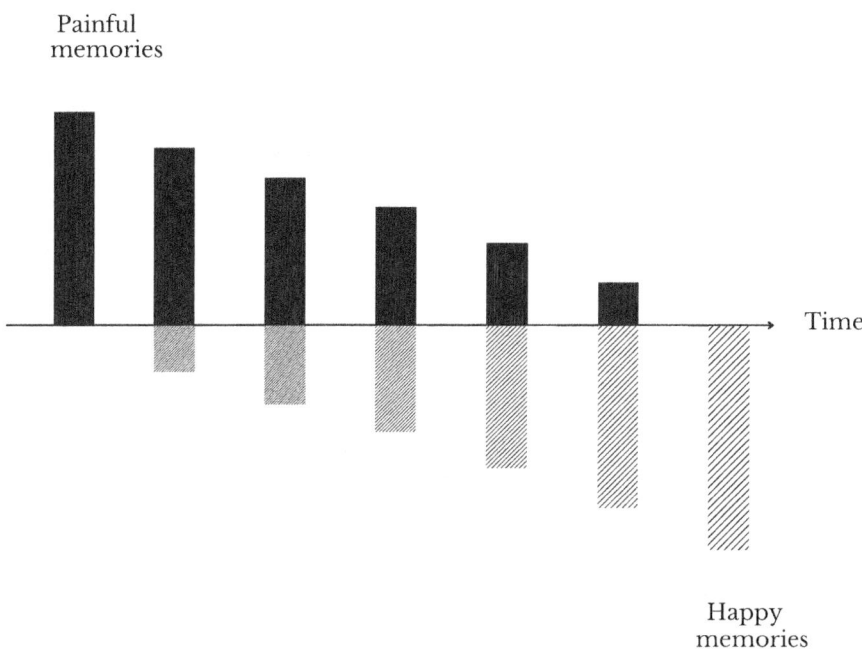

Time is a silent but powerful ally.

At first, the pain may feel unbearable — it can even become physical: a constant weight on your chest, a lump in your throat, a knot in your stomach...
It feels like this mix of emptiness and sorrow will never go away.

But fortunately, you have something precious: **time**.
It won't erase your grief, but it will soften it, helping you turn it into something gentler, something you can carry more easily.

Time doesn't make you forget — and that's a good thing.
It simply allows you to **process** the loss so that it no longer consumes your daily life.

Your pet will forever be a meaningful part of your story, but the sadness will no longer take up all the space.
And you'll learn to live with their absence without letting it define every single day.

Each day that passes is a step forward on your path to healing.
I'm not telling you it's quick or easy — I'm simply asking you to stay hopeful, and to keep in the back of your mind that this pain, no matter how strong, will eventually ease.

Understanding that time is always at work is a beautiful thing when it comes to healing —
because it reminds us that no matter what we do, eventually...
things will get better.

Coping with Grief in Daily Life.

Commemorating.

You want to stop feeling overwhelmed by the pain and emptiness every day. And maybe you've told yourself that the best way to achieve that is to forget your pet — to stop talking about them altogether.

But know this: that's not the solution — in fact, it's the opposite. By doing so, you bury your grief deep inside, at the risk that it will resurface unexpectedly later on.

One powerful way to begin healing is through commemoration. Through simple rituals or meaningful ceremonies, you can honor your pet's memory and give their life the tribute it deserves.

Here are five concrete examples of commemorative rituals:

1. A Funeral Ceremony

When your pet passes away, consider gathering your loved ones to pay tribute. You can give a short speech to thank them, to express your love, and to reflect on how much they meant to you. This kind of ceremony plays a key role in the grieving and healing process.

2. Keeping Some of Your Pet's Belongings

You might feel the urge to quickly get rid of all your pet's belongings.
Don't do that. Of course, you don't have to keep everything, but I recommend holding on to one or two meaningful items.
For example: a collar, a leash, a favorite toy, or a grooming brush.
At first, if these items feel too painful to look at, you can store them in a special place.
Later on, you may feel ready to take them out and use them in small commemorative rituals.
They'll help you keep your pet's memory alive in a gentle, tangible way. You can even include them in a memorial space dedicated to your companion.

3. Creating a Memorial Space

To help you spend intentional, peaceful moments honoring your pet's memory, you can create a special place just for them.
You can place meaningful items there — the ones you chose to keep — along with a small plaque engraved with their name, or even a photo.
This will become a space where you can go whenever you feel the need to remember, reflect, or simply feel close to them.

Did you know there are cemeteries dedicated to animals?
This might also be an option if you're looking for a physical place of remembrance.

4. Planting a Tree

You can care for this tree and watch it grow, while holding a warm thought for your companion.

It's a beautiful example of a memorial space.

This symbolic gesture also gives a sense of continuity to your pet's life — feeding into the natural cycle of life.

5. Creating a Photo Album

Consider creating an album — digital or printed — with a selection of photos of your pet.

You can choose pictures that tell the story of their life by your side: moments of silliness or affection, little mischiefs, walks, birthdays, and of course, photos of the two of you together.

When the time feels right, and you're ready, you can look through this album and revisit the joyful memories you shared.

These are just a few examples of commemorative rituals that can help you manage your grief day by day.

Maybe as you read this, you're thinking, "I don't need any of this." And that's perfectly okay. The most important thing is finding what works for you — what soothes you.

If you feel the need to get rid of all their belongings, then do it.

There's no right or wrong way to grieve.

I'm simply here to guide you and help you move through your grief in a way that feels clear, compassionate, and true to who you are.

Check the ritual(s) you've put in place and describe them.

◯ Funeral:

◯ Keeping their belongings:

◯ Memorial space:

◯ Planting a tree:

◯ Photo album:

◯ Other:

Releasing Your Emotions.

In this chapter, I invite you to explore different ways to express your emotions so you can begin to rebuild yourself after the loss of your pet.

You've been through a whirlwind of emotions, and it's normal to feel disoriented and confused.

Together, we'll see that it's possible to **remember without suffering**.

You'll choose the approach that suits you best.

First and foremost, I strongly encourage you to express your pain — because doing so harms neither you nor others.

There are no side effects to crying or shouting.
On the contrary, it's a way to release pressure and find relief.

It also shows that you are a **courageous** and **strong** person.

So, how can you turn painful memories into happy ones?

1. Therapeutic Writing

An excellent tool for healing.
I encourage you to use the journal provided at the end of this book for that very purpose.

You can write down all the negative thoughts you've been keeping buried inside. Some feelings are hard to express — even to those closest to you — but writing allows you to release them without fear of judgment.

You may not realize it yet, but it's been proven: writing about how you feel helps reduce emotional pain.
Putting your emotions on paper gets them out of your mind, easing that heavy, overwhelmed feeling.

The more you write, the more awareness you gain — and the less it hurts. Because yes, writing helps you organize your thoughts, make sense of them, and better understand what you're going through.
Writing also helps slow down your mind and offers a moment of peace and clarity. It's a form of meditation.

So, as you've probably gathered, I strongly encourage you to write. The pages included in this book are here to support that process — but you can also use your own journal or any other format that works for you. By doing this, your pain will gradually evolve into a calmer, more grounded reflection.

2. EFT
(Emotion Freedom Techniques)

This method has proven to be effective in managing grief.
It helps regulate emotions by combining psychology and
acupressure.
By tapping on specific acupuncture points while focusing on
certain thoughts, emotional blockages can be released.

3. Art

Painting or drawing can sometimes express emotions that are too
difficult to put into words. Music and dance are also powerful
forms of emotional expression. Personally, I've found that coloring
during tough times helped me a lot.

4. Mindfulness Meditation

Mindfulness meditation is simple to practice.
Sit comfortably, close your eyes, and bring your attention to your
breathing.
Give yourself a moment of calm by welcoming your emotions
without judgment.
There are plenty of guided videos and music playlists available to
help you along the way.

Physical Activity

Engaging in physical exercise leads to the release of hormones such as endorphins, dopamine, and adrenaline.
These hormones help reduce stress and improve your mood.
Exercise becomes a healthy outlet for emotional release —
allowing you to channel intense emotions into physical effort
instead of letting them turn into anger or sadness.

Support Groups

There are many support groups dedicated to pet bereavement.
Whether in person or online, they are an excellent resource for
what you're going through right now.
These groups offer a safe space to speak freely with people who
have experienced something similar to what you're feeling.
That makes it easier to express yourself without fear of judgment.

As you can see, there are many ways to release the sadness, the
emptiness, or even the anger you may be holding inside.

As always, I invite you to choose the method(s) that speak to you
the most. Don't hesitate to try more than one.
It's totally okay if you don't find the right fit on your first try —
don't get discouraged. I truly believe that you'll eventually discover
what works best for you.

What is your personal way of releasing your emotions?

....

....

....

What brings you comfort, a sense of peace, or well-being?

....

....

....

Write a sentence that gives yourself permission to feel good. Start with: "I deserve to be happy because..."

....

....

....

A Word for You.

I know that what you're going through right now is incredibly painful. I know you may feel weak, as if you're not handling this storm as well as others seem to.

But I want to tell you something **important**:
It's okay to feel sad, angry, tired, guilty, depressed, and alone.

All of these **emotions** may visit you — during the day, during the night. And that's okay.
It makes perfect sense, because you've lost someone dear and truly **unique** in your eyes.
You have no reason to feel **ashamed**.

I also know that you're feeling **guilty** —
guilty for what you think you didn't do well enough.
You feel responsible for their passing, blaming yourself for not protecting them the way you wished you had. But did you know that during grief, we only see the past through a **filter**?

The filter of sorrow and longing — which gives us a much **darker** version of reality. So instead, remind yourself that you acted from the **heart**, with the information you had, and within your abilities at that time.

You always did your best for them — and they know it.
Just **trust** yourself, the way they always trusted you.
And if you can't do it for yourself yet, then do it for them.
They want to see you just as they always did: with a **smile**.

Some people completely refuse support from anyone — but that's not your case.

I want you to recognize your **strength**.

You're taking initiative by reading and engaging with this book, determined to make it through this dark time.

While some people shut down and suffer in silence, you're doing what it takes to find your way forward.

And if you feel weak or ridiculous, I need to help you see the truth about who you really are.

Weakness is staying alone in the dark, refusing to face the pain, or letting it consume you.

But you — you are not alone. You are not weak. You are not ridiculous.
You are **strong**. You are **brave**.

You're simply going through a difficult time — and you're doing exactly what needs to be done to escape the spiral.

So take a moment to **smile**, even just for a second — as a **tribute** to them.

I know you can do it.

Pet Loss as Experienced by Children.

Losing a pet is a deeply challenging experience for a child.
This difficulty stems from two main factors: a child's limited
ability to fully understand the concept of death, and their
developing ability to express emotions.
That's why it's essential to use language that's appropriate for your
child's age when you have to break the sad news.
Here are some important **guidelines** to follow:

The Truth — and Nothing But the Truth.

One of the most important things when talking to your child is
honesty.
You must be truthful and avoid using vague or misleading phrases
that could confuse or even harm them emotionally later on.

For example, avoid saying:
"He went away"
Your child may begin to associate leaving with death and might
feel guilty when the pet doesn't come back — thinking it was
somehow their fault.

"He went to sleep forever"
This could lead to sleep disorders caused by the fear of not waking
up again.

On the other hand, you can use phrases like:

"He finished his life, and it was beautiful thanks to you,"
or
"He won't be with us anymore, but he will stay in our hearts and memories."

Don't hesitate to use words like death or passing.
They may be abstract for a child, but you can explain that their pet's heart stopped beating and that they no longer breathe.

Also, never try to hide your pet's death from your child.

You might consider replacing the pet with one that looks identical —but doing so would not help them.
They may notice, and it could create even more confusion and emotional distress.

Finally, being honest also means sharing your own emotions.
Don't hide your sadness.
Explain that you miss your pet too.

This will help your child feel less alone and make it easier for them to open up to you.

Communication.

As a parent, you need to do your best to help your child express what they're feeling.

Depending on their age, this can be a challenging task.

Talk about your pet as a family — share fond memories together.

Ask your child regularly if they have any questions, how they're coping, and what they're feeling.

Take the time to answer every question they may have.

There are no silly questions!

A healthy grieving process is one that's expressed.

Loss can lead to changes in eating habits, behavior, or school performance.

Be attentive to these signs, and offer support and understanding.

Your child needs to know they can count on you.

Give them the space to speak if they feel like it.

If these acts of remembrance help you, they will help your child too.

So why keep them from it?

Make Sure They Don't Feel Guilty

Let your child know that they are in no way responsible for their pet's passing.

On the contrary — they helped give their companion a life full of love, and they should feel **proud** of that.

If your child struggles to put their emotions into words, you can encourage them to draw how they feel, or even draw their pet.

When it comes to euthanasia, it's important to give your child the opportunity to say goodbye beforehand.

Explain that the veterinarian will gently stop their pet's heartbeat, which will also end their suffering.

Make it clear that they won't feel any pain thanks to the medication used.

I recommend that your child not be present during the euthanasia itself, as it may be traumatic for them.

The image of their pet's lifeless body could make the grieving process much more difficult.

A Learning Experience.

What I'm about to say may sound surprising,
but what your child is going through right now can actually be
beneficial for their **development**.
In most cases, the death of a pet is the first — or one of the first —
experiences of loss a child faces.
It becomes a powerful **learning moment**.

The child begins to lose a bit of their innocence and starts to
understand what death really means — its finality, and the sense of
absence it leaves behind for those who remain.
This experience also teaches them the value of life.

That's why I encourage you not to rush into getting another pet too
soon. By waiting, your child will come to understand that every
living being is **irreplaceable** and **unique**.

Of course, you can welcome another animal into your home later
on if you wish — but it's important to explain that this new pet will
not be a replacement. They will be different, and together they will
build a new bond. As painful as this time may be for your child,
remember: it is through hardship that we grow.

They will come out of this grief **stronger** and more emotionally
equipped to handle future challenges in life.
Support them through this experience — and help them come out
of it wiser and more resilient.

Understanding Death According to Age.

0–2 years old

At this age, your child does not understand the concept of death.
They notice changes in routine, the absence of someone they love,
and—most of all—changes in your behavior.
It's important to fill that gap with tenderness and affection.

2–4 years old

Your child senses that their pet is gone, but they may believe it will
come back. The irreversibility of death is still an abstract idea.
Be very careful with the words you use, as children at this age may
confuse death with sleep or a trip.
Tell the truth using simple, clear language.
If needed, use pictures or rhymes to help explain.

4–7 years old

They slowly begin to understand that death is permanent.
However, they still believe it can't happen to them or the people
around them.
Many questions may come to mind during this phase.
Answer each one honestly and patiently.
Encourage your child to engage in activities that help them clear
their mind — such as sports, playing an instrument, or drawing.

7–11 years old

At this age, a child's understanding of death becomes much more realistic. They begin to grasp the biological aspects of dying, as well as the different causes of death.

They also understand that death can affect themselves or their loved ones, which may lead to anxiety.

At this stage, you can fully include them in rituals to honor their pet's memory.

11 years and older

A teenager is old enough to understand the more complex aspects of death — including the beliefs, emotions, and fears that surround it. Their grieving process is similar to your own and typically follows the same stages outlined at the beginning of this book.

This is also an age when communication with you might become more difficult. Try to create space for open dialogue — talk together about your pet and face this loss as a team.

It will be beneficial both for their emotional well-being and for your relationship.

I'd like to end this chapter by reminding you that no one knows your child better than you do, and I have no doubt that you'll find the right words to comfort them through this painful experience.

Know that beyond all the advice I've just shared,
your love will be the most precious help they could ever receive.

Tell me what you said to your child when you broke the news.

....

....

....

How did they react?

....

....

....

What did you do to help them express their emotions?

....

....

....

Rebuilding Yourself.

Lessons Learned from Grief.

Here are the lessons I personally learned through the loss of my sweet Bounty — my little furry one, only 6 years old.

My advice to you:

Never stop talking about the **good memories**.
Reflect on everything you did for them and everything you could do. Recognize all the love and care you gave them.
See how **lucky** you were to have known them — and remind yourself that you were the best person for them. You chose each other.

What I came to realize:

Love comes with a price. Would you really prefer never to have known and loved your companion, just to avoid this pain? I wouldn't — they were worth it. Death is **inevitable**. You're **stronger** than you think. Even at your lowest, you can rise again. There is always **light** to be found, even in pain. Your pet will always live on through you. **Thanks to you**, they had a beautiful life.

If someone close to you is grieving the loss of their pet, you now have the power to offer the kind of support you would have needed yourself.

What helped you through your grief?

....

....

....

What made your grief more difficult?

....

....

....

What did this experience teach you?

....

....

....

How did it make you stronger?

....

....

....

Now that we're reaching the end of this book:
When you think about your pet, do you feel less sadness — and
can you see more clearly the happiness they brought into your life?

....

....

....

The Time to Welcome a New Pet.

You've gone through a tragedy by losing your loyal companion, and now you may be wondering whether it's time to welcome another pet into your life. That's a valid question — and one I'd like to help you answer.

The most important thing is to give yourself enough time to properly grieve before even considering it. By now, you understand that grieving isn't about forgetting your pet — it's about not remaining trapped in the pain of their absence.

Why does this matter?
Because as tempting as it may be, rushing to replace your pet just to numb the pain or fill the emptiness they left behind would be a mistake. Take your time, so that when you do decide to adopt again, you're truly ready to open your heart to a new companion.

Your pet was unique — and so was the love you shared. You built a special bond together, and rushing into a new adoption could leave you feeling disappointed.

You may find yourself unconsciously comparing the two, or trying to recreate what you had. But this new pet will never have the same personality. They may be more or less calm, more or less playful, more or less protective.

They are **not a replacement**.

Another risk — beyond making comparisons — concerns the new pet themselves.

A new animal in the home requires time, attention, emotional availability, and affection.

If they sense that you're still in pain, they may absorb your sadness, which could lead to behavioral issues that are difficult to manage.

That's why it's so important to give yourself time to fully **process** your grief.

The mourning process should not interfere with the bonding process with your newly adopted companion.

To know whether you're truly ready to begin a new chapter with another pet, I invite you to reflect on the following questions:

Are you at peace with your pet's passing?

Are you trying to replace them?

Are you ready to accept the difference?

Are you looking to give love?

....

....

....

Why do you want to adopt a new pet?

....

....

....

Don't be too demanding at first — it will take time to build a new bond with them as well.

Choosing a different gender or breed is an excellent way to make a fresh start and help avoid comparisons.

In conclusion, be **honest** with yourself — don't rush.

If you're looking to replace your pet while still in the grieving process, it's very likely that the pain will resurface sooner or later. This won't be good for you, nor for your new companion.

However, if you're at **peace** with your pet's passing, if you've completed your grieving process and you feel hopeful again, then you're probably ready to give love once more.

You know deep down that no other animal will ever replace your loyal companion.

But you'll feel ready to open your heart again.

"If I adopt another pet too soon, I'm neglecting the one I lost."

Getting another pet after a loss is a **delicate** decision, often accompanied by **guilt**. We tell ourselves that replacing them means we didn't truly love or respect them.

But all of that comes down to one thing: the word "replace", which simply isn't the right term.

Welcoming a new pet doesn't mean you're looking to replace the one who passed — it means you're opening your heart to a new and different bond, one that will enrich your life in a unique way. The new pet doesn't replace the old one — it adds to your life, with their own personality, their own way of connecting with you.

You see, love isn't a limited resource. Just because you choose to love another pet doesn't mean you've forgotten the one you lost. They'll always be a part of you, no matter how many new connections you make. By welcoming a new animal, you're not closing the book — you're starting a new chapter in your story.

And remember: there are animals out there in need of loving homes. If you're in a place where you can offer that love, you're giving a truly priceless gift. This isn't about replacing the past. It's about acknowledging the truth: you still have love to give, and another animal is waiting to receive it.

So why hold back?

In truth, it all depends on you. If you feel ready to welcome a new companion but guilt is holding you back, know this: honoring the one you lost has nothing to do with whether or not you adopt again. Giving love to a new animal can bring **happiness** to both of you.

However, if you're hoping a new pet will serve as a bandage to make your grief go away faster, then you may be on the wrong path.

But don't worry — if you didn't have a heart, you wouldn't be here reading these words.

A final word.

Our paths crossed through this book, and I truly hope I've been able to accompany you — even in a small way — through the painful journey of grief.

I want you to know: **I'm proud of you**.

If you've made it to the end of this book without giving up, it means you've done the hard and necessary work to **begin healing**. I hope you're proud of yourself too.

Grieving is a deeply personal and complex process.

There's no right or wrong way to go through it.

So let's take a moment to remember the guiding truths we've shared along the way:

- Take the time you need, and **welcome** your emotions without judgment.

- What you're feeling and going through is completely **normal**.

- Don't wait for someone to save you — you are going to become your **own savior**.

- You may feel like you're drowning in an ocean of tears, fear, and pain. But the only person who can bring you back to the surface is you.

- Don't wait for someone to come pull you out.
- But if someone reaches out their hand — **take it**.

- The importance of rituals.

- The goal isn't to forget — it's to **remember** in order to heal.

- **Acceptance** is your greatest power. You don't need to change reality, you need to face it.

I wish you **strength** and **courage**.

Our animals never truly disappear, because their love stays alive in our hearts.
Honor their memory. Continue to keep them alive through your **memories** — they deserve it, and so do you.

The Legend of the Rainbow Bridge.

To close, I want to share with you this **comforting** and **hope-filled** metaphor often told when grieving the loss of a beloved animal.

The legend of the Rainbow Bridge tells of a beautiful place that exists just beyond this world — a little paradise where animals go after their final journey.

In this place, there is no more pain, no more illness. The nature is lush, the weather is warm and sunny, and peace fills the air.

In this oasis, your companion regains their youth, their energy, and a deep sense of serenity. They play joyfully with other animals, their heart full of love.

But they don't forget you — they wait for you, patiently.

And then, one day, that moment comes.

From the Rainbow Bridge, your animal sees you in the distance — and immediately recognizes you, because the bond you shared is **eternal**.

Then they run toward you with all their strength, faster than ever before, until they reach you.

They leap into your arms, and you cover them with love and affection. With your hearts overflowing, you cross the Rainbow Bridge together.

From now on, nothing and no one will ever separate you again.

This legend offers a peaceful and radiant vision of our companions' departure — and reminds us that **the love you shared will never disappear.**

Appendix.
Your Journal.

This journal is offered as a way to help you never forget them.

If you feel ready, I invite you to fill in these pages.

It is a personal way to **honor** your animal, to move through your grief, and to maintain a lasting connection with them.

Writing regularly in your journal allows you to express your emotions, preserve **precious memories**, and create a comforting routine.

Don't hesitate to come back to your writings from time to time.

Reading them again can offer you a new perspective on your healing journey.

Your Journal.

Paste their photo
right here

Name:

Date of Birth:

Breed:

Male ☐   Female ☐

Date of Passing:

Their Personality Traits:

....

....

....

Your First Meeting:

For example: The first day I saw you...

....

....

....

Your Daily Routine:

....

....

Funny Stories (mischief, quirks...):

Their Favorite Toys/Games:

Your Most Beautiful Memories with Them:

You can write them a letter here.

You may open your heart, share your feelings, express your gratitude, or simply speak to them as you always have.

Printed in Dunstable, United Kingdom